The Arundel Marble

The barcode text reads GW01453064

FRONTISPIECE

Thomas Howard, Earl of Arundel and Surrey (1586-1646) by Sir Peter Paul Rubens. Reproduced by Courtesy of the Trustees of the National Portrait Gallery.

The Arundel Marbles

by D. E. L. Haynes
(Keeper of Greek and Roman Antiquities, British Museum)

OXFORD
PRINTED FOR THE VISITORS
1975

ISBN 0 9000 9019 9

Text set in IBM Aldine. Headings set in Monotype Century Schoolbook

Designed and printed in Great Britain by
Reedprint Ltd., Windsor, Berkshire.

Foreword

The largest surviving portion of the first major collection of Classical antiquities in these islands—the sculptures and inscriptions collected in the early 17th century by Thomas Howard, Earl of Arundel for his London house and garden—is in the Department of Antiquities and many of the best pieces are shown in the Randolph Gallery. Mr. D.E.L. Haynes, Keeper of the Department of Greek and Roman Antiquities in the British Museum is a most distinguished student of their eventful history before they came to rest in Oxford.

Humphrey Case,
Keeper of Antiquities,
Ashmolean Museum.

The Arundel Marbles

Thomas Howard, the first great English art-collector (frontispiece) was born in 1585, the only son of Philip, Earl of Arundel, and his wife, Ann Dacre. Although Philip's father, the fourth Duke of Norfolk, had been attainted and beheaded for treason, Philip himself was allowed to take his place at Elizabeth's court; and the earldom of Arundel, which he inherited in 1580 from his maternal grandfather, Henry Fitzalan, was some compensation for the loss of his father's dukedom. Shortly after 1580, however, Philip incurred the queen's enmity by embracing Catholicism, a step he was persuaded to take by his wife who was herself a convert. In April 1585, when Ann was expecting their second child, some real or imagined threat to his safety induced Philip to attempt to leave the country secretly. Caught at sea, he was brought back to London and imprisoned in the Tower. His son was born three months later.

Philip remained in the Tower until his death in 1595, six years after being deprived of his title and sentenced to death on a charge of having had a Mass said for the success of the Spanish Armada. He had never seen his son. The 'Winter Pear', as the Earl of Essex called the boy, was brought up in the austerely devout household of his mother, who suffered great hardship as a consequence of her husband's attainder, but contrived nevertheless to send Thomas to Westminster School and Trinity College, Cambridge. After Cambridge, Lloyd tells us (D. Lloyd, *Memoires of ... those that suffered,* London, 1677, p. 248), the young man 'traveled to see what they did either in Courts, as at *France* and *Rome;* or in Camps as in the *Low Countries;* or in Universities, as in *St Omers,* etc, from whence he returned a very accomplished gentleman.'

So long as Elizabeth lived, Thomas could not hope to find a proper scope for his accomplishments. After the accession of James I, however, the clouds that had overshadowed his youth began to disperse; and in 1604 James restored him to his father's title as Earl of Arundel. To restore him to his father's estates was beyond the King's power, as most of these had been bestowed already on other branches of the Howard family with whose help James had come to the throne. But Arundel's financial difficulties were greatly alleviated when in 1606, at the age of twenty, he married Alathea, third daughter of the Earl of Shrewsbury, who brought him a considerable fortune. One of the young couple's first acts after their marriage was to buy back Arundel House, the Fitzalan family's London mansion, which Philip Howard had inherited from his grandfather. With its extensive gardens and courtyards, the house occupied a large site on the north bank of the Thames at the east end of the Strand. (Pl. 1).

The first years of married life were filled with the duties and entertainments of the court; but by 1612 Arundel's health was giving cause for concern and he was advised by his doctors to travel abroad. After a brief stop at Spa in the Low Countries he went on to Padua where a stay of some months not only restored him physically but subjected him to the powerful enchantments of Italian civilisation. In the following year he returned to Italy accompanied by his wife and his friend Inigo Jones. In a leisurely tour lasting more than eighteen months the party visited Venice, Padua, Florence, Siena, Rome and Naples, looking at buildings and the great art collections formed by Italian princes and prelates; and it was now, according to Sir Edward Walker (*Historical Discourses* ed. H. Clopton, London, 1705, p. 212), that Arundel 'either took or improved his natural Disposition of being the great Master and Favourer of Arts, especially of Sculpture, Design, Painting and Architecture...' In Rome he took the first steps in the formation of a sculpture collection of his own. With the permission of the papal authorities he carried out excavations in the city and came upon a subterranean building containing a number of Roman portrait statues (Pl. 2). (J. Dallaway *Anecdotes of the Arts*, London, 1800, pp. 256f. On Arundel in Rome see J. Hess in *English Miscellany* Vol. I, Rome, 1950, pp. 197-219. Hess's innuendo, p. 198, that the statues had been 'planted' for Arundel's benefit, is no doubt justified). Wishing to supplement the group, he commissioned the sculptor Egidio Moretti to carve four statues for him in the ancient manner, two wearing the toga (Pl. 3) and two in armour. He also seems to have made his first notable purchase of ancient sculpture at this time, that of the so-called 'Homerus' (Pl. 4), a statue which had already attracted the attention of Rubens (Robert & Erich Boehringer *Homer,* Breslau, 1939, pp. 136-138, p11. 108-113).

On his return to England Arundel began to take an active part in state affairs, with such success that in 1621 James reinstated him as Earl Marshal of England, a hereditary honour of the Howard family forfeited by his grandfather. By this time Arundel had agents buying works of art for him in Italy and most of the other countries of central and western Europe; and Arundel House was rapidly assuming the appearance of an Italian palace, an impression fortified by the addition to it of a long sculpture gallery in the Italian Mannerist style (J. Hess, *op. cit.* p. 200f). In 1616 the sculpture collection was unexpectedly enriched by a generous gift from Lord Roos who, on the point of departing for Spain on a mission from which he was never to return, 'gave the Earle of Arundell all the statues he brought out of Italie at one clap' (T. Birch *Court and Times of James I,* Vol. I, London, 1848, p. 428). How Roos had acquired these statues, we do not know, nor can they now be identified, but we are told that they 'exceedingly beautified his Lordship's Gallerie'. Another gift of sculpture which Arundel received about this time was that of a 'head of Jupiter' from Sir Dudley Carleton, James I's ambassador at the Hague. It was placed 'in his utmost garden, so opposite to the Gallery dores, as being open, so soon as y^u enter into the front Garden y^u have the head in yor eie all the way' (M.F.S. Hervey, *Thomas Howard, Earl of Arundel,* London, 1921, pp. 101-102).

The year of Arundel's reinstatement as Earl Marshal saw an important extension of his collecting activities. Sir Thomas Roe being on the point of departure for Constantinople as James I's ambassador to the Sublime Porte, Arundel approached him to collect ancient sculpture on his behalf in Greece and Asia Minor. (The relevant extracts from Roe's correspondence are conveniently given by Michaelis, *Ancient Marbles in Great Britain,* Cambridge, 1882, pp. 185-204). Roe accepted the commission with good grace and after taking up his post, conscientiously set about making inquiries; but his utter ignorance of what he was supposed to be collecting and his lack of leisure to look for it frustrated all his efforts. Realizing the ambassador's difficulties, Arundel sent out an agent to help him, one John Markham, but this assistant seems to have achieved little or nothing when in 1624, two years after his arrival in Constantinople, sudden death cut his activities short. To replace him, Arundel sent out his chaplain, William Petty, a young man of exceptional energy and resourcefulness, who had probably already had some experience of collecting for him in Italy.

Petty reached Constantinople in January 1625, to be greeted with the news that Roe had just accepted a commission to collect antiquities for a second party, Arundel's hated but powerful rival, the Duke of Buckingham. Embarrassing as this development was, Petty could not afford to alienate the man on whose goodwill he was dependent for the safe-conducts and letters of recommendation he would need; and when Roe proposed that their first discoveries should be shared equally between Arundel and Buckingham, he acquiesced or at least feigned acquiescence. Their first venture in collaboration was an audacious attempt to remove six of the twelve ancient reliefs adorning the propylon added by Theodosius II to the so-called Porta Aurea of Constantinople, originally a triumphal arch of Theodosius I. Although now incorporated in the Turkish castle of the Yedikule (seven towers), the arch and propylon were held in great reverence by the citizens; and the Vizier, the Sultan's Overseer of Works and the Captain of the Yedikule, to each of whom Roe applied in turn, declared that they dared not deface the monument without the Sultan's permission. Nor could the castle garrison be bribed to steal the reliefs, for they feared that the many men and extensive scaffolding needed for the operation would render it all too conspicuous. The ambassador then hit upon the ingenious idea of suborning 'a churchman (i.e. an *imam*) to dislyke them, as against their law', hoping that if the reliefs were condemned as idolatrous, they would be taken down and dumped in some obscure corner, from which they could be safely retrieved later. An *imam* was accordingly engaged for the purpose, but his denunciations fell on deaf ears and the reliefs remained where they were. As a last resort Roe approached the Grand Treasurer, whom he knew to be chronically short of funds, and was agreeably surprised to receive an assurance that the reliefs would be delivered to him on shipboard within a few days. However the Grand Treasurer had reckoned without the superstition of the local populace who believed the reliefs to be enchanted and the safety of the city to depend on them. As soon as they discovered what was in the wind they started to riot, whereupon the Grand Treasurer hastily withdrew his offer and warned Roe that any further prosecution of his designs would endanger his life.

In these intrigues, which lasted well into 1626, Petty had taken little active part, for in May of the previous year he had left Constantinople to make a tour of the west coast of Asia Minor. His first halt was at Pergamon. 'Mr Petty hath bene at the so much famed Pergamo' Roe writes to Buckingham on August 26, 1625, 'and brought somewhat away, as he writes, meane things, not worth his charge, only as testimonyes of his travails; but he is a close and subtill borderer, and will not bragg of his prizes'. From Pergamon Arundel's indefatigable agent went on to Samos, where he obtained more sculptures; but while crossing the narrow straits between Samos and Ephesus, his ship was driven by a storm on to the mainland coast and wrecked. Petty escaped with his life, but his entire cargo of marbles and all his documents went down with the ship; and having no means of identifying himself when he clambered on to the shore, he was arrested as a spy and thrown into prison. However, some Turkish acquaintances presently vouched for him and secured his release; on which he hastened to Chios and engaged divers to salvage the sunken marbles, an operation which was successfully accomplished.

To continue his tour Petty needed new documents, for which he had to apply to Roe. The ambassador received his request with mixed feelings, for it was now quite plain to him that the 'close and subtill borderer' had no intention whatever of collaborating with him or of letting any of his discoveries fall into Buckingham's hands. Moreover obtaining new documents from the Turkish authorities would be an invidious task. On the other hand he had no wish to offend Arundel and he sincerely admired Petty. 'Ther was never man' he admitted to the earl, 'so gifted to an imployment, that encounters all accidents with so unwearied patience; eates with Greeks on their worst dayes; lyes with fishermen on plancks, at the best; is all things to all men, that he may obtayne his ends, which are your lordships service'. In the event the good-hearted ambassador procured the documents and Petty found them waiting for him at Smyrna where he arrived from Ephesus at the end of 1625 or the beginning of 1626.

Here a windfall awaited him. Some time before his arrival a man named Samson, acting on behalf of the Provençal scholar de Peiresc (1580-1637), had assembled at Smyrna a large number of Greek inscriptions from various sources, for which he had paid a total of fifty gold pieces. But just when he was on the point of shipping them, some charge had been trumped up against him, his collection had been confiscated and he imprisoned. Not too scrupulous to profit from another's misfortune, Petty offered a much higher sum for the inscriptions than that paid by Samson and so secured them for Arundel. They included the celebrated chronological inscription from Paros known as the Marmor Parium. (Pl. 5).

From Smyrna Petty proceeded to Athens, where he spent the summer of 1626. Athens was the last stage of his journey and in November, after making arrangements for the shipment of his acquisitions, he set out for home. He had by then, as Roe rather sourly reported to Buckingham, 'raked together two hundred pieces, all broken or few entyre'. The collection reached Arundel House in January 1627. The house must have been amply furnished with sculpture even before the arrival of the Greek consignment. In his *Baconiana* (London, 1679, p. 57) Thomas Tenison relates how Sir Francis Bacon visited it in 1626 and 'coming into the Earl of Arundel's Garden, where there were a great number of Ancient Statues of naked Men and Women, made a stand, and as astonish'd cryed out: *The Resurrection*'. With the arrival of the Greek marbles not only was the size of Arundel's collection greatly increased, but also its scientific interest, for the ancient Greek inscriptions sent back by Petty were the first ever to come to England. Among those present at their unpacking was the famous librarian Sir Robert Cotton, a close friend of Arundel, and so great was his enthusiasm that, though it was the middle of the night, he woke up John

Selden, the *magnus dictator doctrinae nationis Anglicae,* and implored him to start the work of decipherment the very next morning. Selden readily agreed, only stipulating that he should be allowed to enlist the help of the Royal Librarian Patrick Young (Junius) and Richard James. The three worked with such diligence that Selden's *Marmora Arundeliana,* containing twenty-nine Greek inscriptions and ten Latin, appeared before the end of 1628 and spread the fame of the collection throughout learned Europe. A scholar who studied the work with particular interest was de Peiresc, who now learned what had happened to the inscriptions acquired for him by Samson. With rare generosity he declared that he was delighted to find them so worthily published by his old friend John Selden.

Arundel himself had to wait before inspecting his Greek acquisitions. Some months before their arrival in England Charles I had ordered him and his wife to be confined to his mother's house at Horsley in Surrey as a punishment for having failed to prevent a love-match between Henry Frederick, the elder of their two surviving sons, and the Lady Elizabeth Stuart. However, in March 1628 the restriction was lifted and Buckingham's assassination in the following August removed the chief cause of friction between the King and his Earl Marshal. In December Charles and Queen Henrietta Maria confirmed the reconciliation by a visit to Arundel House, where the King inspected all the works with the jealous curiosity of a rival. For, fired by Arundel's example, he too had begun to collect, testifying to 'a Royall liking of ancient statues, by causing a whole army of old forraine Emperors, Capitaines and Senators all at once to land on his coasts, to come and doe him homage, and attend him in his palaces of St James and Sommerset House' (H. Peacham, *The Compleat Gentleman,* 2nd ed., 1634, pp 107f).

Thus Arundel returned to favour; but in addition to the temporary loss of his liberty a crushing fine had been inflicted on him by Charles, which left him heavily indebted for the rest of his life. Though much of his time was still devoted to affairs of state, he found the frivolity of the Caroline court increasingly distasteful and lived more and more for his collection and for the company of the scholars and lovers of art it attracted to Arundel House. Despite his financial difficulties he continued to collect eagerly. Petty had returned to Italy; in 1633 he was even planning a second expedition to Greece, but this came to nothing. A number of letters which Arundel and his sons wrote to Petty in 1636-1637 throw some light on the earl's interests at this period. An antiquity he had particularly set his heart on was that known as the 'Statua' or 'Giulia', the 50 foot high granite obelisk from Egypt which had originally decorated the *spina* of the 'Circus of Caracalla' (Circus of Maxentius) and still lay on the site. But either because the papal authorities refused to sanction its export or because the difficulties of shipping it were too great, it could not be removed—fortunately, since it thus remained in Rome to become the audacious pinnacle of Bernini's Fontana dei Fiumi in the Piazza Navona. Two other famous works which, as we learn from the letters, Arundel greatly coveted, but which he failed to secure, were Signor Pighini's 'Adonis' or 'Meleager', one of the chief ornaments of the Palazzo Pighini near the Piazza Farnese in Rome, and a torso belonging to Jacopo Gaddi of Florence. The Meleager was subsequently acquired for the papal collection and is now in the Vatican (Amelung *Kat.* II, p. 33, no. 10). The torso is almost certainly that of a satyr from the Gaddi collection now in the Uffizi (G. Mansuelli, *Galleria degli Uffizi, Le Sculture,* Vol. I, 1958, p. 155, no. 126). John Evelyn in his *Diary,* November 6, 1644, tells us that Arundel was prepared to pay any price for the Meleager, an observation that lends colour to the accusation levelled at him by Edward Hyde, Earl of Clarendon, that 'his expenses were without any measure and always exceeded very much his revenue' (*History of the Rebellion,* ed. W. Dunn Macray, Vol. I, Oxford, 1888, p. 69). On the other hand, writing to Petty about Gaddi's torso, Arundel expressly instructs him only to buy it 'if to be had for reason'.

By the late thirties of the seventeenth century Arundel House had reached the height of its splendour. At its greatest extent the sculpture collection is said to have comprised no less than thirty-seven statues, one hundred and twenty-eight busts and two hundred and fifty inscriptions, as well as a large number of sarcophagi, altars and fragments. And the sculpture was, of course, only part of what the house could boast. There was a collection of paintings and drawings unrivalled in England except by that of the King himself; there were the rare MSS and incunabula of the Pirckheimer library which Arundel had acquired in Nuremberg in 1636 while leading an embassy to the Emperor Ferdinand II in Vienna; and there were the gems, coins and medals of the celebrated 'cabinet' of Daniel Nys, a collection for which Arundel is reported to have paid the enormous sum of £10,000 when he bought it in 1638. Edward Edwards is not exaggerating when he describes Arundel House (*Lives of the Founders of the British Museum,* London, 1870, p. 195) as an anticipatory British Museum.

Consignments of antiquities continued to arrive up to the eve of the Civil War, by which time Arundel himself had already left England never to return. Deeply disappointed by the King's refusal to restore him to his grandfather's dukedom and now seriously failing in health, he had obtained permission to remain abroad after acting as escort to the Queen and Princess Mary on their journey to Holland in 1642. After spending some time in Holland, where Lady Arundel had already made her home, he went on alone, probably in 1645, to his beloved Padua; and there in October of the following year he died. Evelyn, who visited him six months before his death, gives us a memorable last picture of Arundel in his *Diary* for Easter Monday, 1646: 'I was invited to Breakfast at the Earle of Arundels; I took my leave of him in his bed, where I left that greate and excellent man in teares upon some private discourse of the crosses had befaln his illustrious family; particularly the undutifullness of his grandson Philips turning Dominican Friar, the unkindnesse of his Countesse now in Holland; the miserie of his Countrie, now embroiled in a Civil War, &c; after which he caused his Gentleman to give me directions all written with his own hand, what curiosities I should enquire after in my Journey...'

At the time of Arundel's death most of his pictures and other portable *objets de vertu* were in Holland, where they had been transported in 1643; but the marbles and books were still in Arundel House. By his will Arundel left the whole of his collection to his wife absolutely, but expressed a wish that she should entail it on the heirs of his earldom with a view to keeping it together permanently. Unhappily his hopes were not to be fulfilled. After his death a bitter quarrel broke out between the dowager countess and her son Henry Frederick, the new earl, over money matters; and the breach was still unhealed when in 1652 Henry Frederick suddenly died. Lady Arundel died two years later. She left no written testament, but her favourite son William Lord Stafford, who was present at her death-bed, claimed a nuncupative will entitling him to all her property in Holland, and began to sell the pictures. His right to do so was, however, contested by his nephews, the sons of Henry Frederick, or rather by the younger son, Henry, as Thomas, the elder, who had succeeded to the earldom and lived in Padua, was an imbecile. After some litigation a settlement was eventually negotiated by Sir Edward Walker, formerly Arundel's secretary and a trusted friend of both parties. Henry was confirmed in the possession of Arundel House and its contents and was also awarded Daniel Nys's cabinet of gems and medals. Stafford received all the other property owned by his mother in Holland at the time of her death and also her London house, Tart Hall at Buckingham Gate, together with its contents.

Thus virtually all the antiquities were settled on Henry. The only important ancient work of art to fall to Stafford's share was the life-size bronze head known as the 'Arundel Homer' (Pl. 6), which had presumably been transferred to Tart Hall in Lady Arundel's lifetime. It remained at Tart Hall until 1720 when after the death of William's son, Henry, all the contents of the house were sold and the head was bought by the celebrated physician and collector, Dr Richard Mead. On Mead's death in 1754 it was acquired by the Earl of Exeter, by whom six years later it was given to the British Museum (Walters *BM Cat. of Bronzes*, no. 847). It is now generally accepted that it represents Sophocles.

At Arundel House the marbles seem to have come through the Civil War unscathed, despite the billetting of a Roundhead garrison there in 1646-47. But Henry Howard had not inherited his grandfather's tastes and filled the house, as Evelyn complains, with 'painters, panders and misses', greatly to the detriment of its more venerable contents. The conversion of the upper half of the Marmor

11

Parium into a hearthstone is only one—if the most shocking—of numerous acts of vandalism. Of the two hundred and fifty inscriptions collected by Arundel one hundred and fourteen had already perished when Evelyn, who was on friendly terms with Henry, intervened to save the remainder. 'These precious monuments' he writes in his *Diary* for September 19, 1667, 'when I saw miserably neglected & scattred up & downe about the Gardens and other places of Arundell-house, & how exceedingly the corrosive aire of *London* Impaired them, I procured him to bestow on the *Universite of Oxford;* this he was pleased to grant me, & now gave me the key of the Gallery, with leave to mark all those stones, Urnes, Altars &c; & whatever I found had inscriptions on them that were not Status: This I did, & getting them removed and piled together, with those which were incrusted in the Garden walles, I sent immediately letters to the *Vice-Chancellor* what I had procured, & that if they esteemed it a service to the *University* (of which I had been a member) they should take orders for their transportation'. The offer was gratefully accepted by the University authorities, who conferred academic honours on both donor and intermediary, erected a marble tablet commemorating the benefaction (Pl. 7) and commissioned a lavish new publication of the inscriptions by Humphrey Prideaux (*Marmora Oxoniensia,* 1676). The stones themselves were inserted in the enclosure-walls of the Sheldonian Theatre, there to be exposed to another century of weather and casual damage. When later Evelyn had occasion to inspect them and observed that 'people, approaching them too neare, some Idle people began to Scratch and injure some of them, I advis'd that an hedge of holly, should be planted at the foote of the wall, to be kept breast-high only, to protect them, which the *V. Chancellor* promised to see don next season' (*Diary,* July 13, 1669). It was not until the middle of the nineteenth century that the inscriptions were at last removed to the shelter of the Schools. They are now housed in the Ashmolean Museum.

In 1677, on the death of his brother in Padua, Henry succeeded to the Dukedom of Norfolk, to which Charles II had restored Thomas fifteen years earlier. One of Henry's first acts as head of the family was to obtain permission from Parliament to pull

Arundel House down and divide its grounds into two: the upper part, bounded by the Strand, to be let on lease for residential development, the lower part, next to the river, to be retained as the site for a new family mansion. At the same time Henry determined to dispose of all the ancient marbles still in his possession and presently succeeded in selling a large number of those which had stood indoors to Thomas Herbert, later eighth Earl of Pembroke, who removed them to Wilton House near Salisbury. The pieces in question cannot now be identified, but the majority of them were probably busts, a form of sculpture in which Wilton House is still particularly rich. As no other buyer was immediately forthcoming, most of the remaining sculptures were assembled in the reserved part of the grounds, where they were placed under a colonnade backing on to a new wall built to screen off the site leased for building. When building began here the workmen took to tipping their rubbish over the wall to save themselves the trouble of carting it away; and so much fell on the roof of the colonnade that it collapsed, causing widespread damage to the sculptures underneath. The building site itself had been by no means completely cleared of sculpture; several pieces considered unsaleable had been left behind there and eventually buried in the foundations of Norfolk, Arundel and Surrey Streets. In a letter (Printed in C. Howard, *Historical Anecdotes of the Howard Family,* London, 1769, pp. 91-110) to Lord Willoughby de Parham, President of the Society of Antiquaries, May 10, 1757, James Theobald, a local antiquary, mentions a sarcophagus still to be seen in the cellar of a Mr James Adamson and a broken statue discovered in the cellar of a Mr Aislabie, who had subsequently taken it down to his Yorkshire seat (? John Aislabie of Ripon). In 1891 a marble head was dug up in the foundations of a house in Surrey Street by a builder's workman, who was just disappearing with his prize into the Underground when he happened to be seen by Judge Snagge. Buying the head off its finder for a sovereign, the judge 'jumped into a hansom, and went straight to the British Museum, where it was identified as a fine Greek head of an athlete in Parian marble'. (A. Tilney Bassett, ed. *A Victorian Vintage,* London, 1930, p. 133). It is now in the Ashmolean (Pl. 8). Further sculptures came to light recently when Norfolk and

Howard Streets were demolished and the whole area was excavated in preparation for redevelopment. The new finds comprise a marble head and foot, a Greek funerary inscription, two circular altars, part of a table-support and part of a frieze with Gorgon's heads and consoles (Pl. 9). (On these finds see B.F. Cook in *Transactions of the London and Middlesex Archaeological Society,* Vol. XXV, 1974). The frieze fragment, which is perhaps to be identified with Mr Adamson's 'sarcophagus', was originally in the Duke of Buckingham's collection and must have been acquired by Arundel after his rival's death (J. Harris *Burlington Magazine,* August, 1973, pp. 526-530, fig. 51).

Henry died in 1684 without having disposed of any more of the collection. After his death a few statues were appropriated by his widow, presumably with the acquiescence of her stepson Henry, the new Duke. When, however, four years later her second husband, Lt. Col. Maxwell, attempted to sell them by auction, the Duke intervened on the grounds that they were entailed and had the sale stopped. We may guess that his action was motivated more by dislike of his stepmother than by love of antiquities, for when in 1691 he obtained Parliament's sanction for leasing the rest of the grounds of Arundel House for residential development, he ruthlessly set about ridding himself of all the remaining sculptures. After persuading Sir William Fermor to take the greater part of them at the nominal price of £300, he gave a number of more ruinous pieces to a former family-servant named Boyder or Boydell Cuper and had the residue taken across the Thames to Kennington and dumped on a patch of waste ground beside the river.

Sir William Fermor, created first Baron Leominster in 1692, had his acquisitions taken down to Easton Neston in Northamptonshire, where a new house was then being built for him by Nicholas Hawksmoor. Leominster himself was content to leave the sculptures as they were, despite the damage many of them had suffered in the collapse of the colonnade at Arundel House; but after his death in 1711 his son Thomas, later first Earl of Pomfret, engaged the Italian sculptor Guelfi, a pupil of Camillo Rusconi, to restore them. According to Dallaway (*Anecdotes of the Arts* London, 1800, p. 237), the results were disastrous, for Guelfi, whom Lord

Burlington had brought to England, 'misconceived the character and attitude of almost every statue he attempted to make perfect; and ruined the greater number of those he was permitted to touch'. A detailed description of the disposition of the sculptures at Easton Neston has been left us by George Vertue (*Description of Easton Neston* London, 1758), who visited the house about 1734. Many of the marbles were used to decorate the garden front and a double staircase leading down from it to the parterres. At the end of one of the terraces flanking the garden stood a fantastic pastiche known as 'Germanicus's Tomb', so named because it incorporated a sarcophagus (Pl. 23a) on which, in Arundel House, had been placed a bust supposed to represent this prince. Other sculptures were set at various vantage points in the grounds and a large number were collected in a conservatory where, as we are told by a less reverent visitor than Vertue, there was 'a wonderful fine statue of Tully haranguing a numerous assembly of decayed emperors, vestal virgins with new noses, Colossus's, Venus's, headless carcases and carcasless heads, pieces of tombs and hieroglyphics' (H. Walpole to G. Montague, May 20, 1736). Only a few marbles were admitted to the house itself, and these no further than the entrance hall. Several more, however, were represented in Thornhill's chiaroscuro paintings of the Triumph of Diocletian which decorated the staircase.

The splendours of Easton Neston hardly outlived the first Earl of Pomfret. His son George was already so deep in debt when he succeeded to the title in 1753 that he was obliged to sell all his movable property, and the sculpture collection was bought by his mother, the Dowager Countess Henrietta Louisa, by whom it was presented in 1755 to the University of Oxford. At a solemn ceremony the University returned thanks to Lady Pomfret in a silver casket; a poem composed in her honour was declaimed aloud; and a new publication of the University's sculpture collection, which her benefaction had so greatly enlarged, was entrusted to Richard Chandler (*Marmora Oxoniensia*, 1763). Walpole may ridicule the countess's 'paltry air of significant learning and absurdity', but it was thanks to her that a substantial part of the Arundel collection, comprising some 51 statues, 22 busts and heads and 39 reliefs and other sculptures, was saved from piecemeal dispersal and eventually reunited with the Arundel inscriptions. After more than a century of obscurity in the University's Old Schools (on the ground floor of the Bodleian Library) the Pomfret marbles were gradually transferred during the 1870's and '80's to Cockerell's new University Galleries, the present Ashmolean Museum; and it must have been at this time that, on the advice of C.T. (later Sir Charles) Newton, Guelfi's disfiguring restorations were removed. The collection varies greatly in quality, but it includes some notable pieces, among which we may mention a Greek male torso of about 460 BC (Pl. 10), the well-known Oxford metrological relief (Pl. 11), an excellent Roman copy of a fifth-century Amazon (Pl. 12) and an imposing Roman portrait statue, the 'Cicero' of the Easton Neston greenhouse (Pl. 2).

The sculptures given by the Duke of Norfolk to Boyder Cuper were transferred by their new owner to a pleasure-ground he had opened on the Lambeth embankment, an establishment whose name was rapidly corrupted in popular use from Cuper's to Cupid's Gardens. Here they remained neglected and forgotten for almost thirty years, but in 1719 engravings of 27 of them were published in the fifth volume of John Aubrey's *Natural History and Antiquities of Surrey,* (Pl. 13a), whose editor complains (p. 282f) that 'they received very ill usage from the Ignorance and Stupidity of those who know not their Value, and are still exposed to the open Air, and Folly of Passerby'. It was no doubt this publication which brought their plight to the attention of two friends, John Freeman of Fawley Court, Henley-on-Thames, and Edmund Waller of Hall Barn, Beaconsfield (a grandson of the poet). Through the good offices of James Theobald, whose interest in the antiquities of this area we have already noted, Freeman and Waller persuaded the then owner of the gardens to part with the whole collection for £75 and divided it between them. Of the pieces which fell to Freeman's share and were removed to Fawley Court, eight can still be traced. A draped female statue, and two female portrait heads (Aubrey *op. cit.* Pl. VI, centre, Pl. VIII, top left, top right) are still at Fawley Court, which is now owned by the Divine Mercy College, a Polish Catholic boys' school. The male portrait-statue, Aubrey, Pl. V, centre, was presented to the British Museum in 1845 by W.P. Williams Freeman

(*BM Cat. of Sculpture* No. 1943. The head, which does not appear in Aubrey's engraving, is alien but ancient). The other four pieces are now in the Ashmolean Museum, having recently been deposited there on loan by the Divine Mercy College. They are a circular altar carved in relief with underworld deities, Aubrey, Pl. 1, right (Pl. 13b); the torso of the once celebrated Arundel 'Homerus', Aubrey, Pl. V, right, (Pl. 4) (Haynes in *The J. Paul Getty Museum Bulletin,* 1974), a head of Caracalla, Aubrey, Pl. VIII, bottom left, and a fragment of the north side of the Gigantomachy frieze of the Great Altar of Pergamon (Pl. 14) (Haynes *Apollo* July, 1972, pp. 6-10, figs. 19-15). Of the pieces which Waller removed to Hall Barn only two are still to be seen there: a draped female statue of so-called 'Pudicitia type', Aubrey Pl. VI left, and an Asklepios, Aubrey Pl. VI left (*Apollo* July, 1972, fig. 16).

The waste plot on the Kennington embankment to which the Duke of Norfolk had banished the irreducible residue of the collection had been leased from the Crown by a Mr Arundell, a relation of the Duke's, who acted as his agent. Shortly after the transfer of the marbles the plot was sublet to a timber merchant who planned to construct a wharf at this point and brought over quantities of rubble from the site of St Paul's Cathedral, then in course of rebuilding, to shore up the river bank. During this operation the sculptures gradually disappeared from sight under the rubble and for some years afterwards lay there virtually forgotten. But about 1712 the ground was acquired for building by the father of the Mr James Theobald whom we have already had occasion to mention more than once; and while digging foundations for the buildings, the workmen hit upon a number of the buried pieces, which they disinterred and laid to one side of the site. During the elder Theobald's lifetime nothing more was done about them, but some time after his death Lord Burlington heard of their existence and expressed an interest in them; whereupon James Theobald invited him to inspect them and take away any pieces he wished. Of the several which he chose and removed to Chiswick House, one is still to be seen there: a late Hellenistic funerary relief built into the base of an obelisk in the grounds (*Archaeology,* XXI, 1968, p. 210).

A few years later James Theobald was approached by Lord Petre, who had heard from the Duke of Norfolk that other sculptures might still lie buried on the Kennington site. Though sceptical himself, Theobald readily consented to exploratory borings being made. For six days the excavators worked without success, but just as they were on the point of desisting 'they fell upon something which gave them hopes, and upon opening the ground, they discovered six statues, without heads or arms, lying close to each other; some of a Colossal size, the drapery of which was thought to be exceeding fine...These trunks of statues were soon after sent down to Worksop, the seat of his present Grace the Duke of Norfolk, in Nottinghamshire, where they at present remain'. (J. Theobald *ap.* C. Howard *op. cit.* p. 104f). Unfortunately most of these sculptures seem to have perished in the fire which destroyed Worksop Manor in 1761; but one at least escaped—not a statue, but a fragment of sculpture in very high relief showing a muscular bearded man seen from the back. At the beginning of the present century this piece was recorded by the Worksop historian Robert White as lying in his garden on the outskirts of the town. Later, probably in the twenties, it was mounted on the outside wall of a small cottage close by, where it remained until 1960. But in that year a new tenant moved into the cottage and suspecting that the stone was the cause of internal damp had it taken down. After a vain attempt to sell it to a monumental mason for breaking into chips for strewing on tombs, he offered it to the art-master of a local boys' school as raw material for the sculpture class, but at this point a local antiquarian, Mr William Straw, who realized that it must be an Arundel marble, intervened and persuaded the Worksop Borough Council to buy it. Identified as a fragment of the south side of the Pergamon Gigantomachy frieze (Haynes, *Jahrbuch der Berliner Museen,* Vol. V, 1963, pp. 5-13), it is now in the Worksop Museum.

One other marble from the Kennington dump remains to be mentioned: a column drum which James Theobald took down to his country house at White Waltham in Berkshire, there to be used as a roller for his bowling green. As Michaelis justly comments, *sic transit gloria mundi.*

Plates

Plates

The references to *Michaelis* are taken from *Ancient Marbles in Great Britain* by Adolf Michaelis, translated from the German by C.A.M. Fennell and published by Cambridge University Press in 1882. The entries relating to Arundel Marbles in Oxford, which at that date were housed in the University Galleries (now the Ashmolean Museum, Beaumont Street) and the Ashmolean Museum (now the Museum of History of Science, Broad Street), numbers 1-133 and 156-237 inclusive, appear on pages 540-572 and 580-592.

Plate 1   Detail from a pictorial map of London engraved by W. Hollar, 1646. The detail shows the Strand with the Savoy, Somerset House and Arundel House and part of the River Thames. Photograph by courtesy of the Trustees of the British Museum.

Plate 2   Marble portrait-statue of a Roman wearing a toga. First century A.D. The head is restored. According to J. Dallaway, (*Anecdotes of the Arts*, p. 256), this is one of the statues found by Lord Arundel during the excavations he carried out in Rome in 1613. Ashmolean Museum, Michaelis 45 (formerly Pomfret Collection).

Plate 3   Marble statue of a Roman wearing a toga, probably by Egidio Moretti (c. 1585-after 1651). Ashmolean Museum, Michaelis 46 (formerly Pomfret Collection).

Plate 4   Marble portrait-statue, perhaps of Homer. Hellenistic, second century B.C. Lent to the Ashmolean Museum by the Divine Mercy College, Fawley Court, Henley-on-Thames.

Plate 5   The Marmor Parium, a chronological inscription from the island of Paros, the compiler of which claims that he has "written up the dates from the beginning, derived from all kinds of records and general histories, starting from Cecrops, the first King of Athens, down to the archonship

19

of 'Astyanax (?) at Paros and Diognetus of Athens" (264-3 B.C.). The fragment shown here is in the Ashmolean Museum; another fragment was found on Paros in 1897; the rest is lost.

Plate 6   Head from a bronze statue of a poet. Hellenistic. Traditionally known as the 'Arundel Homer', the head is more probably that of Sophocles. It is often stated to have been found in Constantinople, but there is no evidence for this. British Museum Bronze No. 847. Photograph by courtesy of the Trustees of the British Museum.

Plate 7   A marble inscription set up by the University of Oxford some time after 1670 to commemorate Henry Howard, Duke of Norfolk's gift in 1667 of classical inscriptions 'liberated from Ottoman barbarism' by his ancestor, Thomas Howard.

Plate 8   Head of a youth, marble. Late Hellenistic. Found in Surrey Street in 1891. Ashmolean Museum, 1918 (formerly Snagge Collection).

Plate 9   Marble frieze-block found in 1972 on the site of Arundel House. From a Roman building in Asia Minor. Antonine period. Photograph supplied by courtesy of the London Museum and reproduced by kind permission of His Grace The Duke of Norfolk, E.M., K.G.

Plate 10 (a, b)   Male torso. Marble. Greek, about 460 B.C. Ashmolean Museum, Michaelis 52 (formerly Pomfret Collection).

Plate 11   Marble metrological relief giving a standard length of a fathom (the youth's outstretched arms) and a foot (in the background, left). East Greek, 460-450 B.C. Ashmolean Museum, Michaelis 83 (formerly Pomfret Collection).

Plate 12   Marble torso of an Amazon, an excellent Roman copy of a Greek bronze of about 430 B.C. Ashmolean Museum, Michaelis 24 (formerly Pomfret Collection).

Plate 13a   Plate I from Volume V of John Aubrey's *Natural History and Antiquities of Surrey*, London, 1719, showing two of the Arundel marbles transferred to Cupid's Garden, Lambeth. The circular altar on the right of the plate was

later removed to Fawley Court, Henley-on-Thames, see
Pl. 13b.

Plate 13b Circular marble altar carved in low relief with Hermes,
Demeter and other deities. Greek, late fifth century B.C.
Lent to the Ashmolean Museum by the Divine Mercy
College, Fawley Court, Henley-on-Thames.

Plate 14a Relief fragment from the north side of the Gigantomachy
frieze of the Great Altar of Pergamon. Lent to the
Ashmolean Museum by the Divine Mercy College, Fawley
Court, Henley-on-Thames.

Plate 14b Reconstructed drawing by S.E. Haynes showing the
fragment Pl. 14a between slabs 20.4 and 22.1 of the
Gigantomachy frieze in the Pergamon Museum, Berlin.

Plate 15 Marble Stele of Philista, who is represented with two
servants and a pet-dog. In the background two tomb-
stones, one with a basket on it, the other with a box.
Late Hellenistic. Ashmolean Museum, Michaelis 204.

Plate 16 Torso of youth. Roman copy of a Greek original of the
fourth century B.C. Ashmolean Museum, Michaelis 51
(formerly Pomfret Collection).

Plate 17 The 'Oxford Bust'. A seventeenth century pastiche
incorporating parts of two Roman statues copied from
Greek originals. The head has been identified as that of a
type of Aphrodite. The 'Oxford Bust' served as the
model for G.F. Watt's *The Wife of Pygmalion*. Ashmolean
Museum, Michaelis 59 (formerly Pomfret Collection).

Plate 18 The Muse Clio. Roman copy of a Hellenistic original.
It is thought that this statue may have been the proto-
type of Michelangelo's *Madonna Medici* and Tintoretto's
Sacra Conversazione. Ashmolean Museum, Michaelis 32
(formerly Pomfret Collection).

Plate 19 Portrait statue of a man. Late Hellenistic. Ashmolean
Museum, Michaelis 43 (formerly Pomfret Collection).

Plate 20 Herakles and the Nemean lion. The nymph Nemea sits on
a rock close by holding an oak-wreath, the symbol of
victory. Roman, late second century A.D. Ashmolean
Museum, Michaelis 38 (formerly Pomfret Collection).

Plate 21   Throne dedicated to Isis, Osiris and Anubis by Archidamos, son of Philaenetos. Probably from Delos. Hellenistic, second to first century B.C. The winged griffins on the sides had some influence on English Neo-classical furniture. Ashmolean Museum, Michaelis 87 (formerly Pomfret Collection).

Plate 22   Children revelling: fragment of a Bacchic sarcophagus. Roman, early second century A.D. Ashmolean Museum, Michaelis 107 (formerly Pomfret Collection).

Plate 23a   Marble sarcophagus; Cupids playing with armour. Roman, second century A.D. At Easton Neston this sarcophagus was the centre-piece of the pastiche known as 'Germanicus's Tomb'. Ashmolean Museum, Michaelis 113 (formerly Pomfret Collection).

Plate 23b   Arundel's armorial animals, probably by Egidio Moretti (c. 1585-after 1651). Marble. Ashmolean Museum, Michaelis 124 (formerly Pomfret Collection).

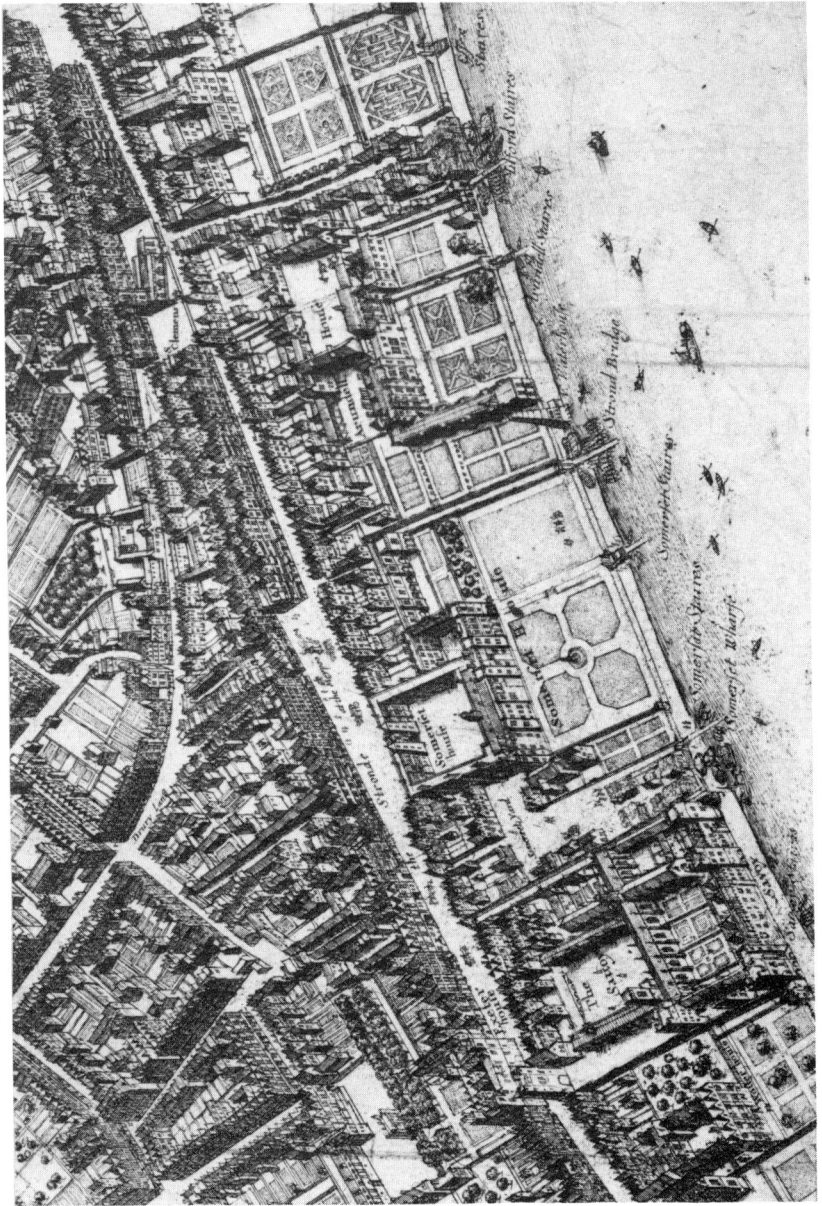

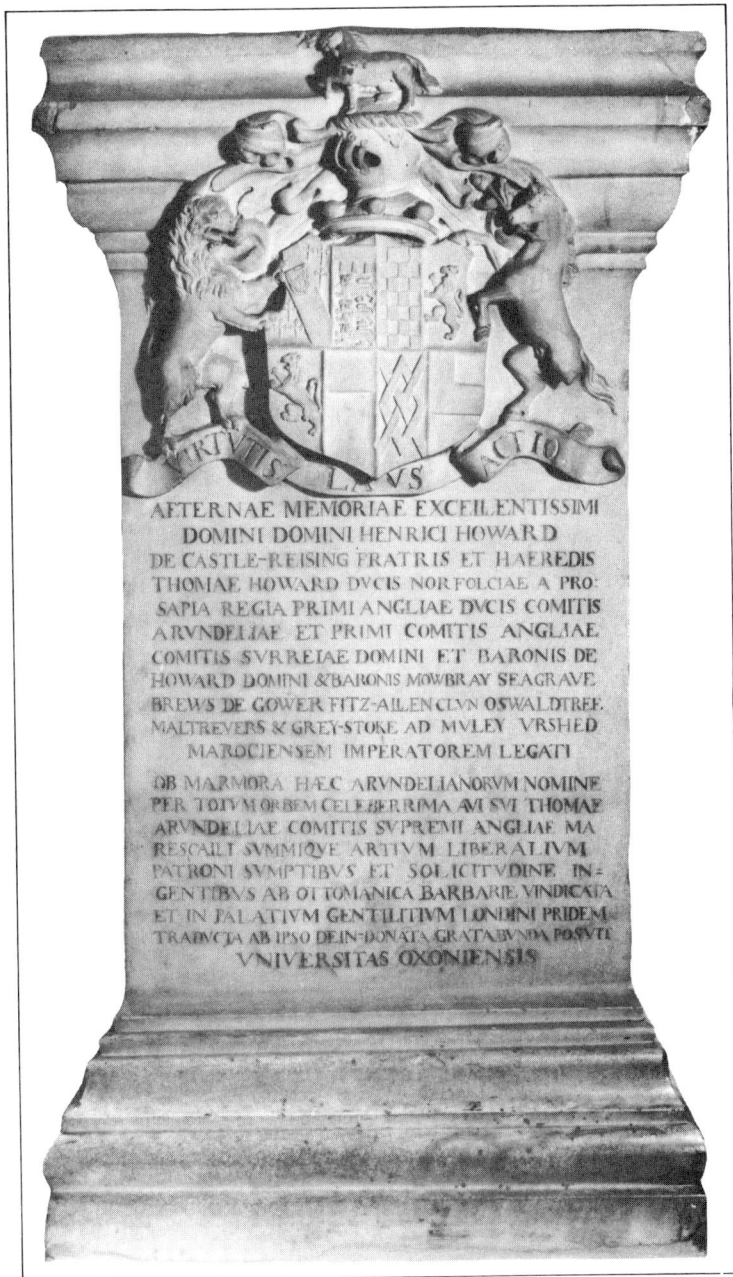

VIRTVTIS LAVS ACTIO

AETERNAE MEMORIAE EXCELLENTISSIMI
DOMINI DOMINI HENRICI HOWARD
DE CASTLE-REISING FRATRIS ET HAEREDIS
THOMAE HOWARD DVCIS NORFOLCIAE A PRO:
SAPIA REGIA PRIMI ANGLIAE DVCIS COMITIS
ARVNDELIAE ET PRIMI COMITIS ANGLIAE
COMITIS SVRREIAE DOMINI ET BARONIS DE
HOWARD DOMINI &BARONIS MOWBRAY SEAGRAVE
BREWS DE GOWER FITZ-AILEN CLVN OSWALDTREE
MALTREVERS & GREY-STOKE AD MVLEY VRSHED
MAROCIENSEM IMPERATOREM LEGATI

OB MARMORA HAEC ARVNDELIANORVM NOMINE
PER TOTVM ORBEM CELEBERRIMA AVI SVI THOMAE
ARVNDELIAE COMITIS SVPREMI ANGLIAE MA
RESCALLI SVMMIQVE ARTIVM LIBERALIVM
PATRONI SVMPTIBVS ET SOLICITVDINE IN=
GENTIBVS AB OTTOMANICA BARBARIE VINDICATA
ET IN PALATIVM GENTILITIVM LONDINI PRIDEM
TRADVCTA AB IPSO DEIN-DONATA GRATABVNDA POSVIT
VNIVERSITAS OXONIENSIS

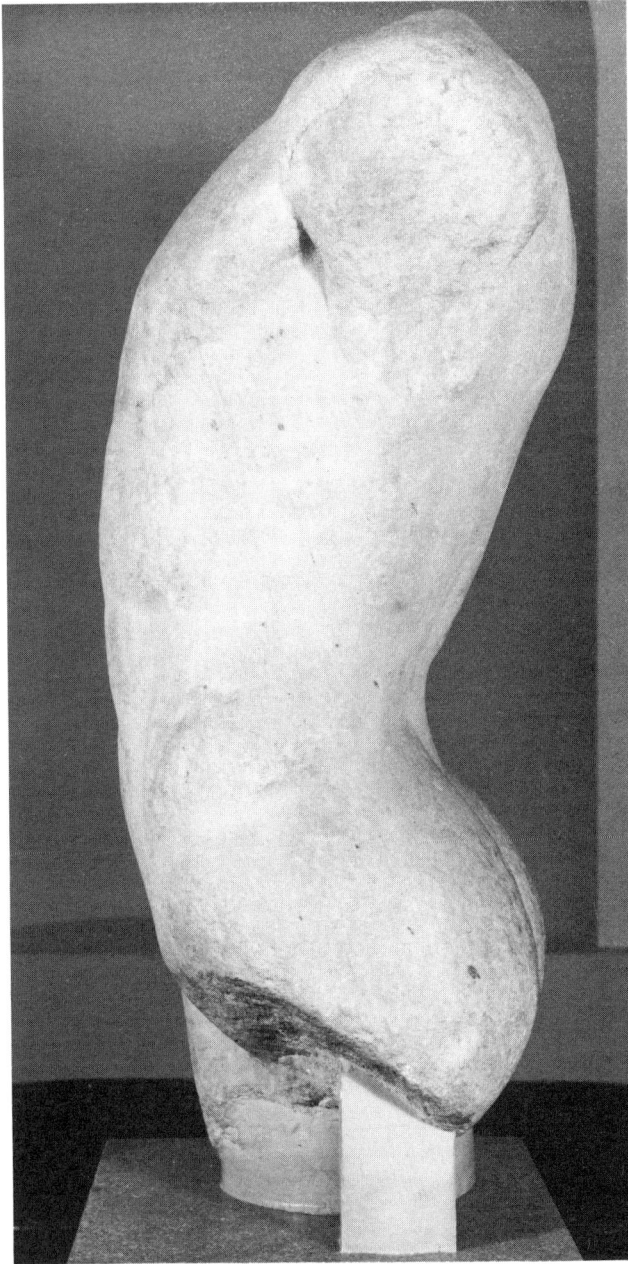

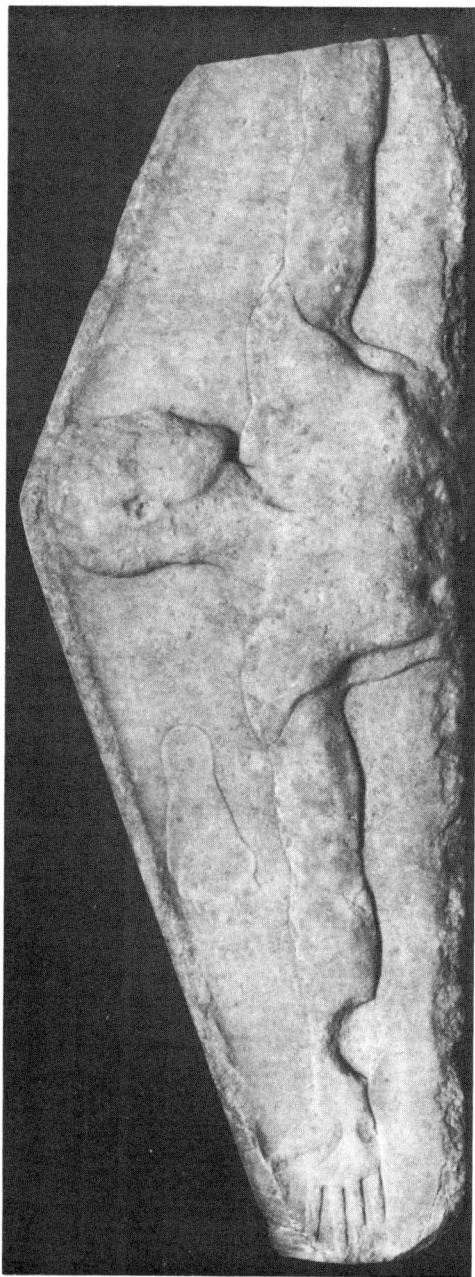

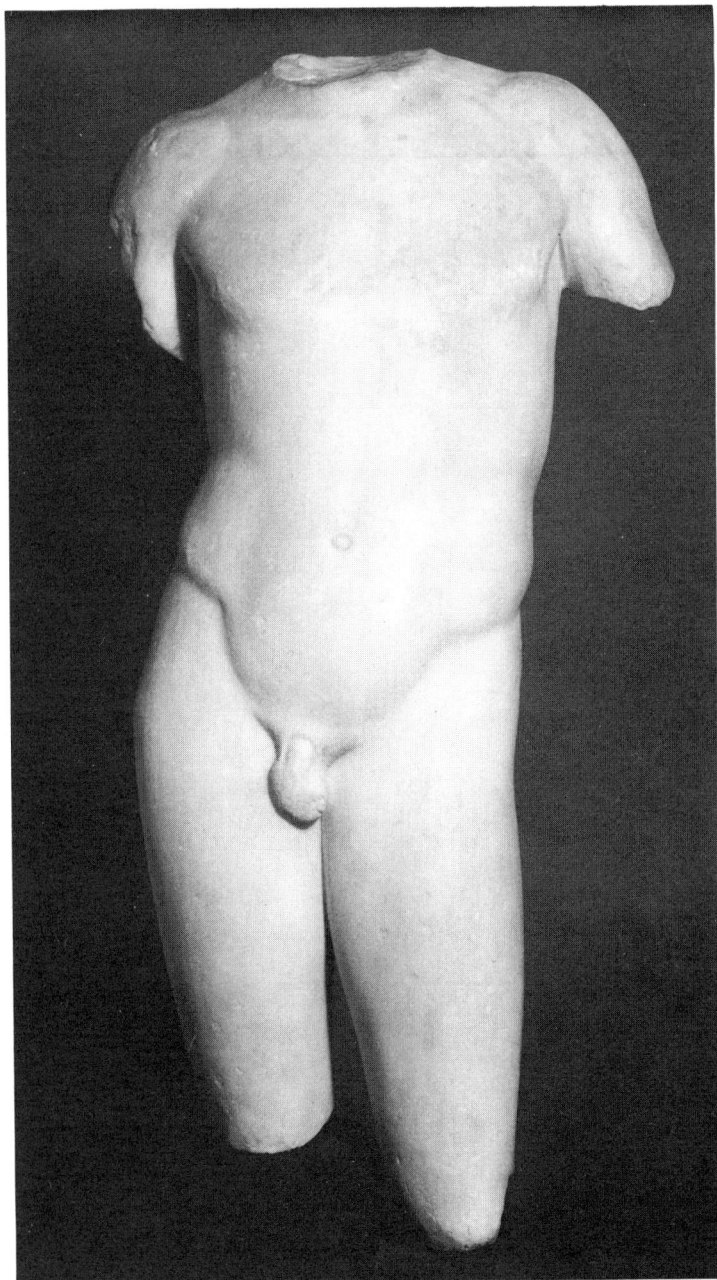

42

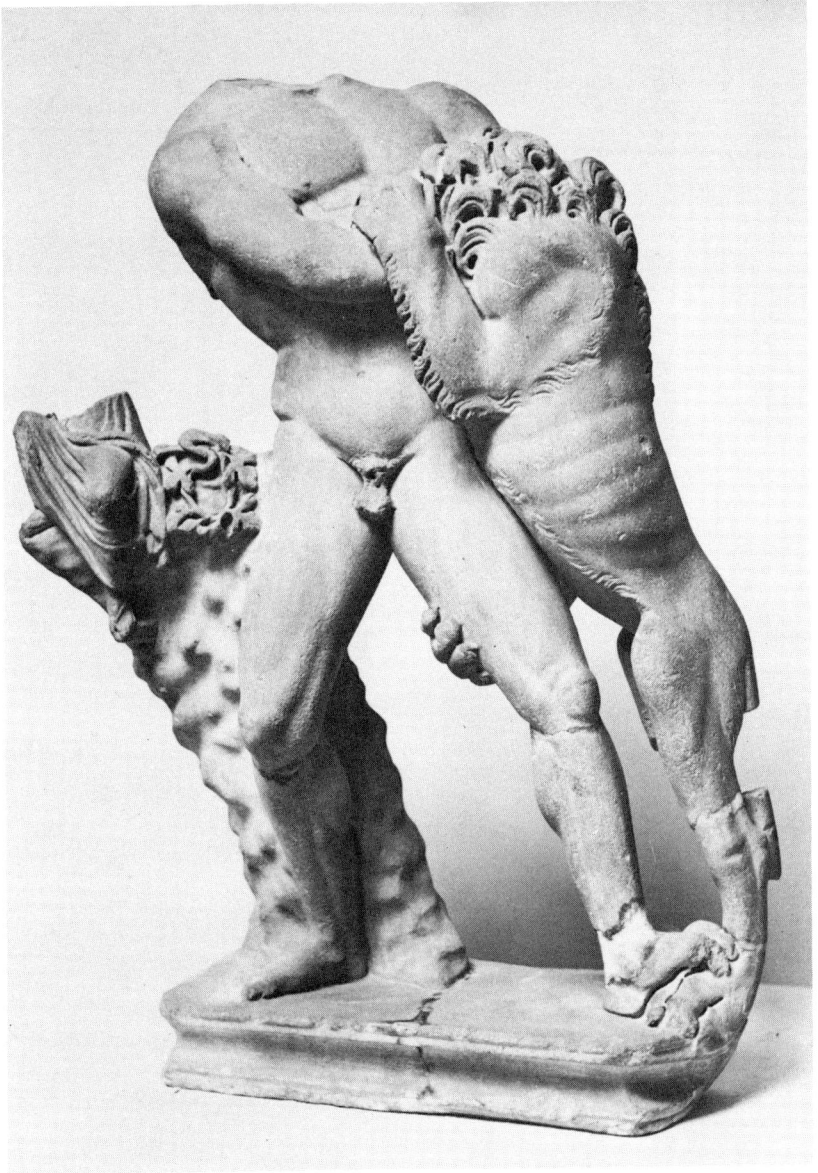

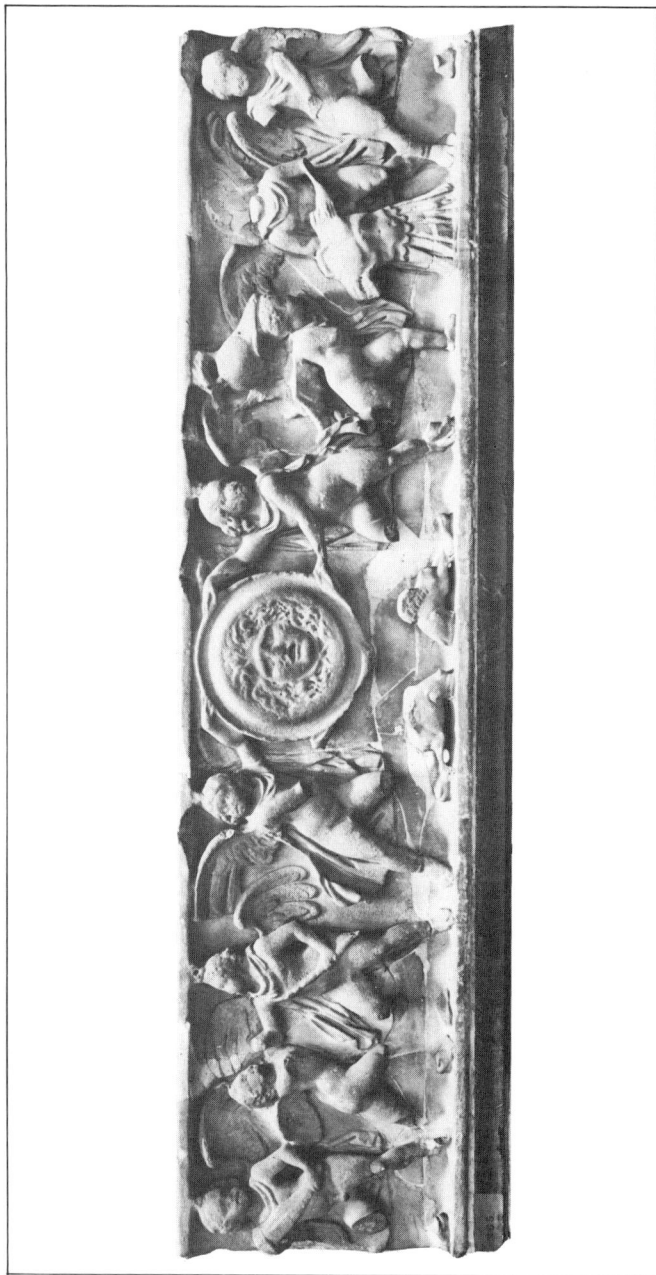